Affordable Care
"Tax"

Affordable Care "Tax"

A GUIDE TO OBAMA CARE (THE ACA)
FOR THE INDIVIDUAL TAX PAYER

Joseph A. Gabra, CPA

LifeRich Publishing is a registered trademark of The Reader's Digest Association, Inc.

LifeRich Publishing books may be ordered through booksellers or by contacting:

LifeRich Publishing
1663 Liberty Drive
Bloomington, IN 47403
www.liferichpublishing.com
1 (888) 238-8637

ISBN: 978-1-4897-0391-0 (sc)
ISBN: 978-1-4897-0392-7 (e)

Library of Congress Control Number: 2015900298

Printed in the United States of America.

LifeRich Publishing rev. date: 1/21/2015

CONTENTS

Affordable Care "Tax":
A Guide to Obama Care (the ACA)
for the Individual Tax Payer

This book is in your hands today because you are someone who loves reading and/or are one of those people who gets befuddled with the complexity of the new Affordable Care Act (ACA) and its relationship with the Income Tax Laws.

For those who love knowledge and search for it, this book will be one of your avenues to learn.

A blind Egyptian man named **Taha Hussein** (1889-1973) was a world renowned historical figure similar to **Helen Keller**.

He was appointed Egypt's Minister of Knowledge in 1950. He led a call for everyone's right to a free education. He said,

> **"Education is as water and air, the right of every human being."**

His revolutionary phrase changed the lives of Egyptians, as he went beyond affordable into free education. Maslow's Hierarchy of Needs fits well with Dr. Hussein's philosophy; Maslow presented human needs as falling into five basic stages: physiological, safety, love, esteem, and self-actualization. Basic needs that comprise the lowest levels of Maslow's hierarchy include security of body, employment, resources, morality, family, property, and **health**. Today in America we need to hear a similar phrase to that uttered by Dr. Hussein:

> **"Healthcare is as water and air, the right of every human being."**

While free healthcare may not be possible, affordable healthcare is indeed a life necessity for Americans especially after the excessive rise of medical costs. We need to consider healthcare as one of the survival needs in the first stage of Maslow's hierarchy.

Working with the Affordable Care Act, right at the initial implementation or earlier, I had the opportunity to discuss the provisions of the law with many opponents.

With all my respect to each opinion, the funniest opinion claimed that the law is one step towards the sign of the Beast and that we have to be on guard to defend ourselves against it. Some people believed that the government will implant a microchip in people that will contain their personal information. Other than that religious opinion and the conspiracy behind it, the other opinions contained concerns that I might agree with if I were in their situation.

But before we go that route, I'm inviting opponents to the ACA to put themselves in a situation where the insurance company re-assesses their premium at an excessive rate or simply denies them because of pre-existing conditions. Imagine how you would feel if you were to run into a catastrophic health issue where you reached the maximum benefit for the year, or for life, and the insurance company stopped your coverage.

Do you still disagree with Obama Care?

We all understand the fact that ACA is a human-made law, which means it's not perfect. The law still needs more efforts to be improved according to the opponent's point of view. If we incorporate these opinions, the law can improve, be strengthened, and reach a successful compromise.

I'm personally experiencing some concerns. I would like the federal government to take into consideration improvements in the practice of the law to ensure equality among Americans when it comes to healthcare.

How This Book is Organized

This book is made up of three main parts. In Chapter 1, I give some background explaining my experience with ACA both as a certified public accountant (CPA) and a certified insurance agent. I also give my argument for why there should be healthcare reform based on the current high cost of healthcare, insurance company capitalism, and the Medicare Part D "Donut Hole". Chapter 2 explains the audience for which this book is intended: the individual tax payer. In this chapter, I introduce individual tax impacts that I expand upon in Part 2 (Chapters 3 through 8). Those chapters cover the following topics: Tax Credit (Chapter 3), Tax Penalty (Chapter 4), the 8 Percent Rule (Unaffordable Coverage) (Chapter 5), the 9.5 Percent Rule (Employer Coverage) (Chapter 6), Filing Status and Dependency (Chapter 7), and Modified Adjusted Gross Income (MAGI) (Chapter 8). Part 3 comprises two chapters. Chapter 9 discusses the new structure for Form 1040 and other new tax forms. Chapter 10 examines several short practical case studies in a question answer format. Finally, I include a conclusion and a glossary of relevant terms.

I wish to acknowledge the help of those who work for the Government of California's Marketplace (Covered California) for their outstanding job performance because they make our job as agents much easier. Many times I was able to solve problems with the new system by speaking with these patient, Helpful, and informative customer service representatives. I would also like to acknowledge Michael A. Owens, PhD, for his assistance with editing and helping clarify the ideas I am sharing here.

To begin, let's revisit the main idea of this book.

CHAPTER 1

Introduction

To understand and interact regarding the main idea of this book:

AFFORDABLE CARE "TAX"

you have to have a clear understanding about the Affordable Care Act.

Background:

Patient Protection and Affordable Care Act (PPACA) is the official name of **Affordable Care Act (ACA).** Decades ago, since the passage of the Medicare/Medicaid Law in 1965, there were many attempts to fix or reform the healthcare system. Finally ACA came into life.

As one of the millions in America who is suffering the inability to obtain health insurance while being denied state supported coverage through the California Medicaid system (Medi-Cal), and also lacking an employer sponsored plan, I watched closely the healthcare reform proposal presented by President Obama, which is why now it's publicly known as **Obama Care.** The proposal was passed in the Senate on December 24, 2009, hours before Christmas, and passed in the House of Representatives on March 21, 2010. Two days after, on March 23, it was signed into law by President Obama.

My journey with the Affordable Care Act started from a personal need for myself and my wife to have healthcare. We were occasionally in need of prescribed medication and unable to visit a doctor for a prescription. Thankfully, the LORD who watches over us and the grace of the LORD was our healthcare coverage for a long time and continues still.

I followed closely on the debate of this healthcare reform among the Senators and House Representatives from both parties. First, I consider the passage of the Senate as a personal Christmas gift. Then I shared the joyful moment with many Americans when it was finally passed the House, as there was no doubt that the President would sign his own proposal.

This was the formation of my initial knowledge about Affordable Care Act, otherwise known as "Obama Care".

Threats from various sources and about fifty attempts to repeal the law notwithstanding, the ACA was upheld by a Supreme Court ruling on June 28, 2012, securing its existence and making the ACA the law of the land. During the ruling, the law was changed to allow States to opt-out of expanding access to Medicaid. Now, not only has the healthcare system changed, but also many aspects in the tax laws have as well.

The next phase of my involvement came because of the ACA direct connection with the tax laws, which is my main focus as a Certified Public Accountant (CPA). This new healthcare reform included many provisions related to how income tax affects individuals, small businesses, and big companies. As with all CPAs, enhancing my knowledge and expertise is my way to secure the public trust and give advice suitable to my clients for their best interest.

My third phase (but not the last one) with ACA was becoming one of the first Certified Insurance Agents in the California Marketplace/Exchange through **Covered California.** A few months after being certified through the Federally Facilitated Exchange (FFE), I began helping residents in the States of New Jersey, North Carolina, Tennessee, and Texas. This year, I added more states by becoming a Certified Agent to assist residents in New York through **NY State of Health** Marketplace.

Dealing with different web-based exchanges has further enhanced my knowledge about the small details in the practice of ACA and of selecting the appropriate plan for each household. My services include educating my clients, helping them in their application process, giving them informative advice regarding plan options available, and finally securing enrollment in any plan of the clients' choice. The first year of implementation didn't run smoothly because of some system errors and administrative or clerical errors among the exchange website and insurance companies, including the Medi-Cal merging process that created more tasks for me to help my clients solving their problems and ensuring their coverage year round.

Although, I wasn't successful with some cases, I am proud to say I found resolution for many others ending my clients' frustrations. Again thanks to the help of Covered California team in that manner.

Now let's try to dig deep into the ACA to get an understanding of the law's purpose.

Why should there be a healthcare reform?

While there are many reasons for the reform, I will focus on what I personally think is reasonable and good ground to have new healthcare system.

A close look into the healthcare system right before the passage of ACA can give you the reason and answer to that question as follows:

- High cost of healthcare

- Insurance company capitalism

- Medicare part D "Donut Hole"

High cost of healthcare:

The high cost of healthcare is a result of:

1. Increase use of technological equipment for treatment and diagnoses increase the cost of treatment,

2. High cost of defensive medication drugs, and

3. High cost of medical malpractice claims and insurance, leading to higher prices for medical services.

These as triangle points of healthcare cost increase lead the insurance companies to raise their premiums to cover up their medical claim payments.

Insurance company capitalism:

This point plays a major factor in the importance of a healthcare reform. Most of the insurance companies run their business in a free market capitalism point of view where profitability is the main focus. In the absence of a governmental role, the insurance companies have the right to:

1. Deny you for pre-existing conditions or drop you when you get sick,

2. Stop treating you when you reached annual or life-time limits, and

3. Increase your premium with no limitations.

In addition to inadequate coverage of the preventive care, as the cost is very expensive, it subsequently leaves their insured member uncovered for those kinds of services.

Finally the confusion regarding the wide variety of plans, some of which include high deductibles and didn't contain essential coverage, makes it harder for the individual to select the right plan.

Generally speaking, only healthy and wealthy people previously could afford to buy health insurance in the old system; even so, they still are not completely protected through the insurance companies. At any moment when you become sick, your company can drop your coverage as well as your business with the insurance company if it becomes unprofitable from their side; why would they keep doing business with you. In the end, you end up paying your medical costs on your own.

The economic analysis before Obama Care recorded that 60% of bankruptcies were related to medical costs. Also, about 50 million people in America were without any medical coverage just because of the affordability to carry health coverage.

Medicare Part D "Donut Hole":

Although the Medicare Law in 1965 created and secured medical coverage for seniors after retirement (which was and is needed the most based on age and health conditions), the law didn't offer enough coverage in regard to prescription drugs, creating a coverage gap known as the *Donut Hole*. While the cost of prescription drugs is getting higher, retired seniors are unable to afford their medication or pay extra out of pocket.

In these regards, ACA provisions are making sure that:

- No one is denied health coverage and everyone is guaranteed acceptance.

- Insurance Companies cannot terminate or stop coverage because of illness.

- Insurance companies must justify any premium increases.

- No annual limits or lifetime limits for healthcare coverage.

- Medicaid will expand the income level ceiling to accept more low income people.

- People in a middle income level will qualify for tax subsidies to afford their premiums based on their income.

- Prevention care is covered in all plans with no co-pay cost (at least once a year)

- A specific time frame is set up for closing the Medicare part D coverage gap.

This is not a complete listing, but it covers the basic ones individuals should care about. I will talk about the other provisions related to the small business and big companies in my next edition.

Until now we have heard news about challenging ACA. On November 7, 2014, the Supreme Court accepted discussing an argument in regard to the legality of Premium Tax Credit for those who enrolled through the Federally Facilitated Exchange (FFE). We are expecting a court decision late June 2015.

If the court agrees, only residents in states that didn't run their own exchanges will not enjoy affordability through Premium Tax Credit (PTC), pay penalties if they didn't carry insurance coverage, or being exempt from the penalty if the premium cost reaches a certain level of their income.

Away from political and judicial arguments we are continuing to abide by the law while we wait to receive other direction.

The Affordable Care Act has the following characteristics:

- Categorization

- Eligibility

- Predictability

Categorization:

The beneficiaries of ACA can be categorized as retired and non-retired; retired individuals will benefit through ACA's closing of the gap in Prescription Drugs Part D in their Medicare coverage.

The non-retired can be categorized based on their income: low, moderate, or high.

Low income people have benefits through Medicaid expansion up to 133% of the *Federal Poverty Level* (FPL) or up to 138% after adding 5% disregarded income in some states. Additionally, the Medicaid system will accept two more beneficiary types:

1. Legal aliens not yet residents formerly denied Medicaid full coverage (emergency only) can now enjoy full coverage.

2. Childless people ages 25 – 64 years old without dependents formerly denied coverage are now covered.

9

Although it is not the case in all the states, the ACA is attempting to set unified rules for all states in this regard; however, the Supreme Court ruling of 2012 sent it back again to the discretion of each state.

Moderate income people (138% - 400% FPL) can find quality affordable cost coverage through the Federal subsidy paid on their behalf to their current insurance company.

High income people over 400% of FPL, as they can afford to pay their own premium, are not eligible for any tax subsidy. Although they feel they are the only losers from the law, they also benefit from ACA's protection of unreasonable premium increases, guarantees of acceptance, and removal of annual and/or lifetime limits.

Eligibility:

When I speak about eligibility, I mainly am talking about the *Premium Tax Credit* (PTC). That part of the law assures the affordability concept of the healthcare insurance premium.

Many people become confused when it comes to their income or eligibility to enroll in the Marketplace/ Exchange. If your income is above 400% you are not prohibited from enrolling in the Marketplace/Exchange. In addition, if you are offered insurance through somewhere else (such as your employer), you are still free to shop in your state or federal Marketplace/Exchange.

Think about when you are shopping for a Christmas gift: You are free to shop everywhere to pick and choose your favorite item. Some people receive a discount based on criteria you may not meet to make you eligible for the discount, but again, you're still able to shop and pay the full market rate.

The bottom line is that everyone is eligible to enroll in the Marketplace/Exchange. What differs from one income level to another are the circumstances that can make you eligible for Premium Tax Credit or not.

I will explain in detail about Premium Tax Credit later.

Predictability:

Predictability of an income you didn't earn is yet a major characteristic of ACA. The enrollment process in your federal or state Marketplace/Exchange includes a question about your income. Many people have gotten confused because ACA starts its first year enrollment for 2014 on October 1, 2013. At that point, no one had yet completed their 2013 income tax. Also, one of the proofs of income at the time was previous year's tax file; at that moment the only available tax file was 2012. So the question was: Which year's income were they asked about? The 2012 income level (past year), the 2013 income level (present year), or the 2014 income level (next year)?

The answer for that question is your 2014 income level, which is based on information about your recent income and the prediction process in that system, assuming no change to that income for the whole year until you report a change of income once it has happened to reflect in your health insurance the amount of tax credit you're eligible for. The same thing will happen for each enrollment year. When we predict the income of the year we are enrolling for while we don't know if it will increase, decrease, or stay the same by the end of that year.

My advice here is to be aware during the year of any change of income and report it to your Marketplace/Exchange through your agent just to avoid any tax penalties from the IRS for *underestimated* income.

CHAPTER 2

Individual Tax Impacts

Background:

Most people assume that the Affordable Care Act (ACA) started in the 2014 tax year. The answer is yes on the healthcare insurance side, while at the individual tax level there were a couple of changes in the income tax law as it relates to ACA before 2014.

In this chapter I will talk about:

1. The changes Affordable Care Act reflecting on the individual level through income tax or medical costs from when the law was signed (2010) and what to expect in the tax year 2014 and thereafter. (Chapters 3-8)

2. The new structure for Form 1040 and new tax forms and worksheets related to individual tax to assure Affordable Care Act tax compliance. (Chapter 9)

Changes on the Individual Tax level

Let's look at the beginning of Affordable Care Act timeline:

- Year 2010:

    Those retired people who reached their $2,830 out-of-pocket expenses for their individual Medicare Part D have received back $250 to reduce that cost in a process to close the Medicare Part D prescription drug coverage gap.

- Year 2011:

    1. Long-term care insurance programs will reimburse some cost of home and nursing home care.

    2. A fifty-percent discount on Brand-Name drugs was added as a further step to close the Medicare Part D gap.

- Year 2013:

    1. Investment income tax on the individual level rose 3.8%. The surcharge was imposed on investment income (e.g., interest, dividends, capital gains, royalties, rents, etc.) above a

certain level of income as shown at the table below.

Tax Filling Status	Threshhold
Single or Head of Household	$200,000
Married Filling Jointly	$250,000
Married Filling Separately	$125,000
Qualifying widow(er) with a child	$200,000

2. Medicare Health Insurance tax of 2.9% increased 0.9% on earned income over the same level of income as shown at the above table.

3. The medical expenses disallowed threshold as an itemized deduction had been increased from 7.5% to 10%.

   For example: if your Adjusted Gross Income (AGI) is $ 100,000 and you spend $12,000 during the year for medical reasons, you previously could deduct from your income $4,500 ($12,000 - $100,000*7.5%), while starting 2013 you could deduct only $2,000 ($12,000 - $100,000*10%). The exception is that those over 65 years old can still deduct medical expense above 7.5% of income through 2015.

Now we return to our main focuses, which is tax year 2014.

An individual must obtain "Minimum Essential Coverage" to avoid a penalty. The penalty is not the only coming change to this tax year, and thereafter many other rules will follow when it comes into Affordable Care Act regarding Income Tax, such as:

- Tax Credit (Chapter 3)

- Tax Penalty (Chapter 4)

- The 8 Percent Rule (Unaffordable Coverage) (Chapter 5)

- The 9.5 Percent Rule (Employer Coverage) (Chapter 6)

- Filing Status & Dependency (Chapter 7)

- Modified Adjusted Gross Income (MAGI) (Chapter 8)

Each of these items will be discussed below.

CHAPTER 3

Tax Credit (Premium Tax Credit)

I will start by discussing the Premium Tax credit to encourage and motivate more people who are still waiting and watching to join the millions who enjoy the peace of mind through Affordable Healthcare Insurance, with the support of the Federal Government to subsidize that cost of their premium by paying a part of it to the insurance company of their choice.

Only seventeen states have implemented a state run exchange, adopting the law from the start, while the rest of the states run through what is called the Federally Facilitated Exchange (FFE). Of those who run through the FFE, 27 States also opted-out of the Medicaid expansion based on the 2012 Supreme Court ruling. Six other states have taken a variation on the approach by partnering with the federal government. No matter which approach your state took, the way you shop for insurance everywhere is the same.

In the beginning of the implementation on October 1, 2013, we all thought that as long as you purchase health coverage throughout the year 2014 and you are under a certain limit of income guidelines, you are eligible to receive a federal subsidy to assist paying your premium called the *Premium Tax Credit* when you file 2014 taxes. This is a new *REFUNDABLE* tax credit you can only receive that credit in advance in a monthly bases in case you purchase your insurance coverage through the Marketplace/Exchange, while you will receive the PTC at the end of the year if you obtain your coverage directly from your insurance company. This turns out to be incorrect; I will disclose these details later.

The dilemma here is that the IRS issued Publication # 5120 (Rev. 4-2014) giving facts about the Premium Tax Credit and setting the eligibility for that credit as follows:

The Premium Tax Credit Eligibility

You may be eligible for the credit if you meet all of the following:

- **buy health insurance through the Marketplace;**

- **are ineligible for coverage through an employer or government plan;**

- **are within certain income limits;**

- **do not file a Married Filing Separately return;**

And

- **cannot be claimed as a dependent by another person.**

As we see here, the first condition is to buy your insurance **through the Marketplace.** The government drops the right of that tax credit to a person with a grandfathered plan under the same Income guideline or another who bought his insurance directly from the insurance company.

In my opinion these situations are rare, as most people already enrolled through the Marketplace/Exchange have immediate savings in their premium, while the grandfathered-plan-insured members already could afford to buy insurance a long time ago before the Affordable Care Act and have kept their insurance. My expectation is that they have it through their employers or they are the high income level, which means that even if they participated in the Marketplace/Exchange they are not qualified for the Premium Tax Credit. If in this case it happens that the person still qualifies for a tax credit based on his household income level and has kept a Minimum Essential Coverage (MEC) for the whole year out of the Marketplace/Exchange, I think there will be a dispute with the IRS regarding their eligibility for the premium tax credit.

Not only this, but we learn about another piece of conflicting news regarding the Premium Tax Credit eligibility.

"On July 22, 2014, the *District of Columbia Circuit Court of Appeals* **and the** *Fourth Circuit Court of Appeals* **reached conflicting outcomes after considering whether the premium tax credits are limited under the law only to individuals who enroll in qualified health plans through state-based Health Insurance Exchanges. The DC Circuit ruled that the tax credits are** limited to individuals who enroll in state-based Exchanges, while the Fourth Circuit upheld IRS rules that also include individuals enrolled in federally-facilitated Exchanges. **A final resolution of the issue has not yet been reached.**

"So, the IRS Guidance states that, at this time, **nothing has changed regarding the tax credits, and the credits remain available**. **Whether enrolled in coverage through a federally-facilitated or state-based Health Insurance Exchange, individuals do not need to take any additional action or make any changes in response to the court rulings"** (HR360 blog, 2014).

On November 7, 2014, the Supreme Court accepted another challenge in regard to the legality of the Premium Tax Credit for those who obtain their coverage through FFE. In my opinion this step will help to end the previous conflict.

We are waiting for a new ruling which will deny or allow the taxpayers in some states enrolled to keep this new tax credit, while there is no threat or effect on those who live and receive their coverage through their own state Marketplace/Exchange.

How does Premium Tax Credit work?

The way that the tax credit works currently has changed the method people shop for insurance. You will never get an accurate quote unless you go through the whole application process through your State or Federal Marketplace/Exchange.

To explain further, as with any regular insurance, everyone asks his/her agent to give a quote before giving away their personal information, which is smart. With the new Marketplace/Exchange system, however, it doesn't work that way. In most cases the quote comes out inaccurate because the regular calculator attached into the Marketplace/Exchange website drops many factors and comes up with an estimate not related to the facts of the applicant and his/her household.

Some Certified Insurance Agents (CIA) felt like that mistake, especially here in California early in October 2013, was at the time when the Covered California Marketplace/Exchange website wasn't completely ready. The calculator tool was meant to be a tool for estimating purposes.

For example: the calculator came with an estimate for 2 household members with an average income of $35,000 based on their age and zip code showing a tax credit of around $700 monthly to bring their premium down to $175/month for both of them.

In an actual household situation, an older person (higher cost) may already have insurance coverage, and the cost for the younger is actually a little over $200, a cost which is considered to be affordable with no premium tax credit.

Therefore one important fact to consider in shopping for health insurance for you and your household is that once you input the correct information in the Federal or State Marketplace/Exchange, to ensure that the quote you will receive is the accurate one that will not change (in other words, the same plans, same companies, and same premium) because it is one Marketplace/Exchange channel no matter whether you do it on your own, use the help of a Certified Agent, a Certified Councilor, or others.

To know how it works, you need to understand how the Affordable Care Act mandate regarding the cost of Health Insurance Premium related to income level.

2014 Federal Poverty Level								
Household Size	100%	133%	138%	150%	200%	250%	300%	400%
1	$11,670	$15,521	$16,105	$17,505	$23,340	$29,175	$35,010	$46,680
2	$15,730	$20,921	$21,709	$23,595	$31,460	$39,325	$47,190	$62,920
3	$19,790	$26,321	$27,312	$29,685	$39,580	$49,475	$59,370	$79,160
4	$23,850	$31,721	$32,914	$35,775	$47,700	$59,625	$71,550	$95,400
5	$27,910	$37,120	$38,517	$41,865	$55,820	$69,775	$83,730	$111,540
6	$31,970	$42,520	$44,120	$47,955	$63,940	$79,925	$95,910	$127,880

Let's assume we have two single taxpayers – 25 years old and 50 years old – earning the same level of income as shown below. The regular premium without tax credit $200 for the young and $500 for the older person. The table below will show the calculation of the premium and tax credit in each income level.

Income Level as % of FPL	Premium Cost as % income	Earning By year	25 Years old		50 Years old	
			Premium	Tax Credit	Premium	Tax Credit
*100% – 133%	2%	$15,000	$25	$0	$25	$0
133% – 150%	3% – 4%	$16,513	$69	$131	$47	$431
150% – 200%	4% – 6.3%	$20,423	$88	$112	$88	$412
200% – 250%	6.3% – 8.05%	$26,258	$157	$43	$157	$343
250% – 300%	8.05% – 9.5%	$32,093	$200	$0	$234	$266
300% – 400%	9.5%	$40,845	$200	$0	$323	$177
** + 400%		$55,000	$200	$0	$500	$0

*In that level of income, each of them qualify to be under their State Medicaid System in State of California called Medi-Cal. The premium costs we see in that line can be called Share of Cost not yet practically implemented. Still, in some states there is $0 cost for state Medicaid coverage, while other states do not even accept to expand their system guidelines.

No Tax Credit is applied here, and the person does not qualify to any Federal assistance as it should be a State level of responsibility.

**Over 400% of FPL earner is not eligible to receive tax credit.

To understand the concept of affordability, you have to ask yourself

What is the actual cost of your insurance premium?

An agent who behaves like a salesman will tell you the net cost after your tax credit to show you what a good deal he/she is offering you, meaning you could pay more premiums. In contrast, a professional agent will lay the truth and all number regarding your case and advise you not to use all of your credit in a way which will affect your tax liability by the end of the year.

But why pay more when you have the opportunity to pay less?

Everyone needs to understand that the calculation of the premium tax credit is calculated based upon your income. Surprisingly, some agents thought they could use the lesser of the income from tax year 2012 or 2013. The income level you need to use is your actual income, and the Marketplace/Exchange will assume that as your 2014 provisional income is your income for the whole year. That estimated provisional income will be used to figure the amount of tax credit you are eligible for, and you can use it in advance. That is the predictability characteristic.

During the year many changes to your income can happen that will affect your tax file at filing time.

For example, Peter (25 years old and single) earns $16,500. His premium cost is $200/month, and he is eligible for a tax credit of $135/month. His affordable premium now is only $65/month. Because of his honesty at work, his employer is slightly rewarding him, allowing him overtime, a bonus, and a promotion. Peter's income increase shows on his W-2 as a total of $22,000, and that means his premium tax credit eligibility is less than what the IRS paid to the insurance company. At that point, they will recapture the balance in his income tax.

Here the actual cost for his insurance is $2,400/year ($200/month), and he will pay the affordable amount based on his income $780/year ($65/month), only the amount that he can afford. The Federal government subsidizes his cost, paying on his behalf the amount of $1,620/year ($135/month) to the insurance company.

In the example above the extra tax liability my not exceed $300. Although it is an extra cost, it is not harmful.

Let's see another case where the premium before the credit was $1,250 and after the credit came down to $150, meaning you obtain a total of $13,200 for the year and got to the point that when you prepare your income tax, you find out that you are not eligible for that credit. You could be considered as underestimating your income, so a penalty and interest may apply over and above the amount you owe. How hard is that? And what is the real cost of your insurance premium?

So to really know your health insurance cost you should wait to make the final calculation until your accountant prepares your income tax and see if what you have already paid for the health insurance during the year is enough, more, or less of what you should pay. In this situation you will be at one of three positions:

- Pay extra cost because your income was higher than assumed (extra tax payment)

- Receive extra credit because your income was less (extra tax credit) less cost.

- Pay nothing receive nothing because your income level was the same as assumed.

As a tax professional, I know that many of us will guide our clients into using the Premium Tax Credit as an extra tool we can offer them to help avoid an excessive tax liability at tax time. This new tool could be added to our tax planning strategy. For that reason, if you are Certified Insurance Agent, you should ask our clients to consult their tax professional to see to what extent they can utilize their Premium Tax Credit before you enroll them.

CHAPTER 4

Tax Penalty
(Shared Responsibility Payment)

One of the main reasons why some people abide the law is to avoid a penalty. Although that was not the official name, most people will come to this conclusion when they are required to pay their *Shared Responsibility Payment* (SRP).

This is simply saying that when an individual does not have a *Minimum Essential Coverage* (MEC) for at least nine months, he/she is responsible for amount of payment determined at the tax filling and added to his/her tax liability.

The amount of that payment will be based on how many people in the household were not covered and for how long. The released information for the Certified Insurance Agents was limited to basic details, while the real calculation released to CPAs and Tax practitioners are greater in details.

We will discuss in detail that calculation for the public to understand and make an informed decision about the cost and benefit of having insurance coverage, for those who are self preparers who didn't get the chance of knowing the deep details about the Affordable Care TAX, and for the Certified Agent dealing with the insurance aspect only to introduce valuable advice to their clients who are considering an opt-out and who are willing to sacrifice an extra payment.

Some agents and tax preparers know the basic numbers regarding the Penalty:

Tax Year	Greater of		Maximum
	Income percentage	Amount per person	
2014	1%	$95 / Adult $47.50 / Child	$285
2015	2%	$325 / Adult $162.50 / Child	$975
2016	2.5%	$695 / Adult $347.50 / Child	$2,085
2017 & after	*Figures will be adjusted for Cost Of Living*		

While everyone thought that the Maximum of the penalty for the household will not exceeds $285 for year 2014.

Here is how the tax year 2014 penalty is laid out by the IRS:

The greater of:

- o 1 **percent of your household income** that is above the tax return filing threshold for your filing status, or

- o Your family's **Flat Dollar Amount**, which is $95 per adult and $47.50 per child, limited to a family maximum of $285,

- • The greater of the above two factors is capped at the cost of the **National Average Premium** for a bronze level health plan available through the Marketplace/Exchange in 2014. For 2014, the annual national average premium for a bronze level health plan available through the Marketplace/Exchange is **$2,448 per individual** ($204 per month per individual), but $12,240 for a family with five or more members ($1,020 per month for a family with five or more members).

So from here I can tell you that the penalty will be calculated in three steps:

1. We will calculate the percentage of your household income after the filing threshold.

2. Multiply the household size by the Flat Dollar Amount per each adult and child stopping at the maximum level.

3. Using the greater of step 1 & 2 and making sure it should not exceed the **National Average Bronze Plan Premium (NABPP)** $2,448 / individual annually.

Particularly for 2014, comparing the 1% to the Flat Dollar Amount will result in using the 1% calculation because the maximum level of the Flat Dollar Amount will never be greater than the percentage figure. Also for 2014, the 1% will never exceed NABPP for this year unless your income is more than $200,000 per year.

Be aware: Based on the above calculation it seems that the actual amount of payment will mainly be based on the duration of non-coverage. The 1% here is the key figure to know. Whether one household member or all household members are not covered, the penalty remains the same: 1% of the household income. That figure will then divided by 12 and the result multiplied by the number of months without coverage.

The challenge we are facing here and which is not yet clear, where in a household situation we have two members without healthcare insurance coverage, one of them for a period of five months while the other for seven months.

What is the penalty calculation would be?

I personally have an answer for a complicated case like that, but we all waiting for an answer and guideline from the IRS into that matter.

These calculations have two variables: the first one is the filing threshold. The table below shows 2013 and 2014 just to show the changes from each year based on Cost Of Living; we don't have these number for 2015 or after.

Filing Status	Age	Filing Threshold 2013	Filing Threshold 2014
Single	Under 65	$10,000	$10,150
	65 or older	$11,500	$11,700
Head of Household	Under 65	$12,850	$13,050
	65 or older	$14,350	$14,600
Married Filing Jointly	Under 65 (both spouses)	$20,000	$20,300
	65 or older (one spouse)	$21,200	$21,500
	65 or older (both spouses)	$22,400	$22,700
Married Filing Separately	Any age	$3,900	$3,950
Qualifying Widow(er) with Dependent Children	Under 65	$16,100	$16,350
	65 or older	$17,300	$17,550

The second variable is the NABPP. That number will vary each year based on statistics obtained from the

Marketplace/Exchanges all over USA and the IRS will make it available in its guideline to allow the accurate calculation for the SRP.

National Average Bronze Plan Premium (NABPP) Table for 2014

Number of Months	Family Size				
	1	2	3	4	5 or more
1	$204	$408	$612	$816	$1,020
2	$408	$816	$1,224	$1,632	$2,040
3	$612	$1,224	$1,836	$2,448	$3,060
4	$816	$1,632	$2,448	$3,264	$4,080
5	$1,020	$2,040	$3,060	$4,080	$5,100
6	$1,224	$2,448	$3,672	$4,896	$6,120
7	$1,428	$2,856	$4,284	$5,712	$7,140
8	$1,632	$3,264	$4,896	$6,528	$8,160
9	$1,836	$3,672	$5,508	$7,344	$9,180
10	$2,040	$4,080	$6,120	$8,160	$10,200
11	$2,244	$4,488	$6,732	$8,976	$11,220
12	$2,448	$4,896	$7,344	$9,792	$12,240

From the table above you can tell that the calculation is going in monthly basis. Your employer, the Marketplace/Exchange, or your insurance company will report the duration of your coverage to the IRS. For those who have coverage for partial year, the calculation will consider the gap in your coverage during the year.

Example 1:

David, a 30 years old single person in the year of 2014 with $45,000 income, does not have MEC for 6 months during the year. Calculate his penalty as follows:

- First subtract his filing threshold from his income $34,850 ($45,000 - $10,150) and find one percent of it: $348.50.

- David's flat dollar amount is $95.

- David's annual national average premium for 2014 is $2,448.

- Since the percentage of the household income ($348.50) is greater than the Flat Dollar Amount ($95) and less than the NABPP ($2,448), David's shared responsibility for the 6 months gap in coverage is $174.25 ($348.50/12 month * 6).

Example 2:

Sam & Sylvia, a married couple filing jointly with 1 child over 19 and 2 children under 18, have an income for 2014 of $85,000 and didn't have any coverage for the entire year. The calculation of their penalty is as follows:

- First subtract his filing threshold from his income of $64,700 ($85,000 - $20,300). One percent of it is $647.00.

- Sam & Sylvia's flat dollar amount is $380 ($95 * 3 adults + $47.50 * 2 children), which is greater than the $285 per family, so the flat dollar amount will be at the maximum $285.

- Sam & Sylvia's annual national average premium for 2014 is $12,240 ($2,448 * 5).

- Since percentage of the household income ($647) is greater than the Flat Dollar Amount ($285) and less than the NABPP ($2,448 per person), Sam & Sylvia's shared responsibility is $647.

Some people choose not to buy health coverage based on the cost of their premium, agreeing to face the penalty not knowing the exact calculation. In my opinion, even if you can afford to pay the penalty (which may appear less costly than buying insurance), you are carrying the risk of being un-insured the whole year, and the cost of an un-expected event may be more costly than the cost of premium you are trying to avoid. As we all know, medical costs without insurance have already driven some people in the past to lose a lot or decide to declare bankruptcy. Also, the first year tax penalty is fairly small while in the following years it becomes very costly. Think about health insurance in the same way you would think about the auto or home insurance you have. It is required you have it by law even though you mostly don't use it, but when an unpleasant event happens you have the peace of mind of knowing **YOU ARE COVERED.**

One more important issue in the event you are self-employed: The cost of your health insurance premium is deductible from your gross income. This means your insurance premium is already paid for from your gross income.

But this situation is not final. While there is a penalty, there is a free admission, meaning there is a way to waive that tax penalty. In other words, you can get an exemption to pay your Shared Responsibility Payment (SRP). Two different sources are available to approve the exemption: through your Marketplace/Exchange or through the IRS. It's no wonder here if I say that the Marketplace/Exchange can give you the exemption because not only those who didn't have MEC or did not participate in the Marketplace/Exchange needs the exemption but there are some cases who partially participated is indeed in need for it as well.

If you got your exemption from the Marketplace/Exchange, you will receive **Exemption Certificate Number (ECN)**. Your agent should be your helper in that case, while your tax professional will help you to get your exemption through the IRS.

Here are some options in qualifying you for this exemption:

- Income level is under certain amount

- Coverage is considered unaffordable

- Short coverage gap

- Certain noncitizens

- Members of a health care sharing ministry

- Members of Federally-recognized Indian tribes

- Members of certain religious communities

- Hardships

This book does not discuss all of the above situations. Generally for individuals, you have two main options which I will discuss here:

First: Your income level is equal to or less than 138% of FPL, meaning you are qualified to enroll at your state managed health coverage Medicaid even if you did not participate or your state didn't allow you because it chose to opt-out.

Second: Your health insurance premium costs more than 8% of your income, so you can opt-out of buying health insurance and still be exempt from paying the penalty. This is what I personally call the 8 percent rule.

CHAPTER 5

The 8 Percent Rule
(Unaffordable Coverage)

As per IRS Publication 5172,

"The individual shared responsibility provision of the Health Care Law requires you and each member of your family to:

- Have qualified health insurance, also called minimum essential coverage,

- Have an exemption, or

- Make a shared responsibility payment when filing your federal income tax return."

The second option for the taxpayers is having an exemption I mentioned above, and Publication 5172 shows that there are several ways to get you qualified for that exemption. In this part we will talk about the 8 Percent Rule. If the level of premium expense for your Minimum Essential Coverage exceeds 8% of your household income, your coverage is unaffordable; you have the right not to buy health insurance coverage, and you still are going to have an exemption, meaning you will have NO SHARED RESPONSIBILITY PAYMENT.

In this part I need to guide the public to be aware of the wording "Minimum Essential Coverage." Do not assume that because a plan you like would cost more than 8%, you can ignore the fact that there is a less costly lower level plan with a higher deductible that may cost less than the 8% of your household income. In that case you might be subject to the Shared Responsibility Payment.

Please don't assume, but rather consult your agent and your tax accountant to get the right advice.

Also remember that you might build up your decision based on your recent income level at the time of open enrollment, while after the open enrollment your income may increase to a level which will disqualify your household from the exemption. (Predictability of your income in beginning of the year may be less than actual income at end of the year.)

For example:

Chris is a taxpayer shopping for health insurance during the open enrollment period and has found that his premium would cost him 8.2% of his household income, so he decided not to buy insurance for that year. Later on, right after the open enrollment period ended his income increased a little in a way that would not qualify him for what is called a **special event** to enroll during the year, while the amount of his income change affected the cost of the premium compared to the income relative to his insurance to drop under the 8% threshold. If he wouldn't qualify for any other exemption he is under the Shared Responsibility Payment obligation.

Just to mention, a hardship is one of the options for the exemption. I will notate here that in hardship cases the 8 Percent Rule is expanded. A household qualifies for a hardship condition if two or more family members' aggregate cost of self-only or employer-sponsored coverage exceeds 8% of total household income, the same as the cost of any available employer-sponsored coverage for the entire family. A family under a hardship can be exempt from the paying Shared Responsibility Payment.

As you see here, not only the premium cost of one person is considered, but the 8 Percent Rule considers the cost of two or more household members, which might be happening with most families.

But wait, is that what we need to accomplish to avoid the penalty?

From a CPA's perspective, maybe yes. Our job is to dig deep into the laws to use all legal avenues to find your exemptions, while as a Certified Agent, our main focus is to ensure that you and your family are being COVERED.

CHAPTER 6

The 9.5 Percent Rule
(Employer Coverage Level)

Another issue that may cause some people to put themselves under a big tax liability is when they aren't aware of (such as when they self-enroll) or when their agent didn't confirm whether the rule applied to them.

Simply put, the Affordable Care Act is meant to exist to cover those who have no one to offer them health coverage. If your employer or workplace offers a group health insurance, that law is not directly for you. While it made some improvements in the general health insurance coverage you already have, ACA mainly expanded the coverage to those whose workplace does not offer that benefit.

Generally speaking here, the Federal government plays the role of a huge company, and the entire citizenship and residents are effectively its employees. Thus, the Affordable Care Act is a group insurance plan that makes sure that the entire population is covered and afforded their health insurance coverage. If your own company insured you or offered you that benefit, you are considered to have affordable coverage.

Based on your income level, when you are shopping around and find out that your premium after the federal subsidy will be more affordable than your employer sponsored coverage, you may assert your right to buy through the Marketplace/Exchange ONLY if the premium cost of the **Minimum Essential Coverage** through your employer cost you more than 9.5% of your combined household income for the year.

For example: if your income level is at $60,000 and your premium cost through your employer sponsored group plan cost you $220 every paycheck biweekly, that means the premium cost for your insurance for the whole year is $5,720 ($220 * 26 periods), so your premium is 9.533% of your annual household income. Now you are qualified to get your insurance through Marketplace/Exchange and are eligible for Premium Tax Credit based on your household income and family size.

In that case above if we assume that your spouse is making any amount above $1000 making your household increase above $61,000 it will lower the cost of your employer health insurance compared to your combined household income to a level below the 9.5% and it will disqualify you from the Premium Tax Credit and thereby you will have to pay back this amount in your tax return.

That is why I turned away many clients advising them that in the long run the real cost of their employer sponsored plan will be less costly than that of the Marketplace/ Exchange one because as we remember the real cost is the cost without the tax credit.

Some agents misunderstand that concept saying if you have employer sponsored coverage you are not qualified to enroll in a Marketplace/ Exchange plan. The only thing you are not qualified for here is the Premium Tax Credit. You still can qualify to shop and compare through your state and Federal Marketplace/Exchange (Eligibility Characteristic). If we carefully and accurately fill out our Marketplace/Exchange application, we will avoid this dilemma; however, sometimes innocent mistakes can lead into a disaster at tax time.

Further, there is a larger issue now regarding this specific rule when it comes to spouse and dependent coverage through the employer sponsored plan. Most employers when they offer health coverage to their employees offer it at a discounted rate as a benefit to their employees while they also offer the same coverage to their spouses and dependents at no discount so when they shop at the Marketplace/Exchange they are not eligible for a tax credit as the calculation of 9.5% goes through how much the employee cost compared with the household income. That cost will not exceed the percentage required by law while it easily does it for the spouse premium cost.

So let's assume the employer offers to all its employees a 50% discount which the employer will carry on the rest of the premium, meaning that in no case the cost of the employee premium exceeds the 9.5%, while the cost for the spouse and dependents is unaffordable. In that case, the spouse and dependents are neither supported through the employer nor through federal sponsored coverage. They still are able to buy from the Marketplace/Exchange only if the premium cost with no tax subsidy is considered less.

In some cases, when the employer offers the health coverage to the employee at $0 cost, if we add the 100% cost for the spouse and dependents combined, it might balance out the total cost of health coverage to the household income.

So, in this regard I would like to suggest a slight improvement to the actual practice of the law by expanding the Premium Tax Credit to include the household when the combined cost of the health coverage through employer is over the 9.5% of the combined household income.

For now, never give up contacting a certified agent to find out your options. Couple months ago, I was able to help a family of five end up with a huge savings by taking the spouse and children away from the unaffordable employer-sponsored plan.

CHAPTER 7

Filing Status & Dependency

Filing status and dependency are major points of health insurance coverage. It could affect your income negatively, adding a huge tax liability burden.

As per IRS Publication #5120 (Rev. 4-2014) mentioned above, the last two criteria for Premium Tax Credit eligibility are that taxpayers:

- **do not file a Married Filing Separately (MFS) return; and**

- **cannot be claimed as a dependent by another person.**

Filing at the Marketplace/Exchange as Married Filing Jointly (MFJ) will qualify your household for the PTC and the advancement of it (the APTC). If at tax season you and your spouse change your mind and decided to file as MFS for any reason, you will automatically be disqualified for the Premium Tax Credit, meaning that all the advanced payments you received will be recaptured back creating a huge tax liability with a tax penalty and raising the real cost of your health insurance. This final point is a real call to awareness to all married taxpayers.

If necessary, please put aside your disagreements as a couple and come together at the tax season to avoid losing tax benefits. This Premium Tax Credit is a big issue which has reached in some families to over $13,000 per year. Please consult your accountant before you consider any change in your married filing status.

Also the dependency situation is a confusing point. We all know that children 19 to 24 years old and full time students supported by their parent more than 50% of the year are considered by tax law as dependents of their parent. People need to be careful of these issues in their Marketplace/ Exchange application because you could lose benefits or you could create more liability.

For example:

On January 1, 2014, Shawn and Sandra include their 23 year old son Matthew in their health insurance plan through the Covered California application. Based on their income level and household count, they received $700 monthly as a premium tax credit. During the month of April, Matthew dropped classes and moved out of the home for the rest of the year, meaning that he was no longer considered a dependent. If Shawn and Sandra didn't act actively with their Agent to change the household situation, they would get to the point with their accountant at tax season where they would face a recapture of part of the credit.

The problem in this case is that although the Marketplace/Exchange reports the household enrollment in a monthly basis, does the IRS? Will it change the dependency in a monthly basis as well? That will be one of the questions we are looking for an IRS response to. Also regarding the dependency matter, you can add a friend as a dependent on your tax file if they meet the dependency requirement. In this case, you can add them in your health insurance application. Again, we come to the predictability characteristic, which says that I'm applying now and my friend lives with me and I'm supporting him with more than 50% of his expenses during the year. If before a six months period ends, my friend moves away, he is no longer considered to be a dependent of mine. At this point we need to be actively reporting any change of the household situation regarding someone who has moved in or out as it affects both Income Tax and Health Insurance.

As we see from all of these situations, the health insurance industry in regards to practicing ACA and its relationship with income tax has made major changes in the way you shop for coverage. The changes of your household during the year require that you keep a very close communication between you, your agent, and your tax preparer. Eventually you need service in your coverage during the year to reflect any change of circumstances in your life. Any delay of these changes will appear in your income tax file, hopefully in a positive side giving you extra credit, while we are looking to avoid any negative ones thereby requiring you to pay extra tax liability. Please keep contacting your agent and your tax professional during the year for advice.

Modified Adjusted Gross Income (MAGI)

For the purpose of preparing tax we use that expression to calculate the extra tax called the *Alternative Minimum Tax (AMT)* by recalculating your AGI by adding back some deductions and non-taxable items. The new figure is called the *Modified Adjusted Gross Income (MAGI)*.

For health insurance and Medicaid purposes only, we are using same phrase, but in another way of calculation. This point is related directly to the previous point we discussed in Chapter 7.

I would like to differentiate between both of them by calling the first type of income modification the **Taxable MAGI** and the other modification the **Healthcare MAGI**, especially in my case as a CPA and Certified Insurance Agent who deals with both of them at the same time.

Note that some of those who meet certain criteria to qualify for Medi-Cal that Healthcare MAGI rule will not apply to them.

We all know about Adjusted Gross Income (AGI), that number in your income tax line 37 form 1040, line 21 form 1040A, or line 4 form 1040EZ (whatever form you used for your tax). That AGI is your gross income from all sources after we deduct certain allowable deductions. We call it the above the line deductions.

For ACA calculation purposes, we have to modify that AGI to get that new Healthcare MAGI income base. To get the idea, you need to remember that in all our talk we mention the phrase HOUSEHOLD Income. AGI by itself in most cases is not the household income.

For example:

In a family of four, I have a husband and wife filing their tax with an AGI amount of $75,000. They have two children, one a full-time student less than 24 years old making $6,000 from a part time job. The other child, 18 years old, earned $2,500. The amount of $6,000 and $2,500 are not included in the parents tax file and may or may not be filed or reported to the IRS as it is considered under the threshold filing requirement.

However, the MAGI for the household should be $83,500 ($75,000 + $6,000 + $2,500) adding total income of the household members for the health insurance to calculate the Premium Tax Credit (PTC) and/or Sharing Responsibility Payment (SRP).

Adding the total income of all household members is not the only figure to determine the MAGI, but it is considered the main factor because it applies to most households, while the other is not a common one.

Other MAGI factors add back to the AGI items like:

- Tax Exempt Interest:

  The IRS gives tax break to encourage the taxpayers investing in a local or municipal bond by allowing exemption in taxing the interest received or accrued from that source. Although it is shows in your tax reporting but it is not included in your AGI, so it is added back for Healthcare MAGI purposes.

- Non-taxable Social Security benefit:

  As we all know, based on the income level, some of the Social Security benefits are taxable. Also the non-taxable portion of this benefit needs to be added back to your AGI to obtain our new Healthcare MAGI.

- Foreign Earned Income and its related housing expense:

  The IRS gives another tax break to those who work and live in foreign countries under certain conditions and exempt that income from being taxable. That income will not appear in their AGI; so it needs to be add back to figure Healthcare MAGI.

Basically, you need to estimate your Healthcare MAGI at the time you are applying in the Marketplace/Exchange and adjust it during the year instead of having income tax surprises at year end. This is what we consider Tax Planning.

CHAPTER 9

The New Structure for Form 1040 and New Tax Forms

Form 1040 and new forms

This 2014 tax year will be full of new changes related to Affordable Care Act implementation.

New questions will be asked of all the areas of new tax credit, new tax liability, and how to figure if you received extra or less credit. Do you have to pay the responsibility payment or are you are exempt? Were you offered Minimum Essential Coverage (MEC) through your employer? Is it affordable to you?

Many questions still need answers, such as how do the CPAs and other tax preparers keep up with all of that over and above their many questions regarding individual tax files?

I'm personally expecting a delay in 2014 tax filing and the refund process. New forms will be coming to complete your tax file in regards to the Affordable Care Act. There will be new forms, and there might be mistakes that would get the IRS system completely overloaded not only with Affordable Care Act (ACA) implementation, but also with the implementation of Foreign Account Tax Compliance Act (FATCA) which was signed as law in the same time with (ACA) March 2010 and implemented in the same tax year 2014. Each new law added extra forms to the filing process. We know that the IRS system is able to handle it all; the issue appears to be with the public confusions dealing with many new forms. That's why we are expecting that the filing process could be harder for the self-preparer, so educate yourself more about the new changes or seek professional help. Don't rely only on the software, at least in the first year.

Now we will explore the changes of the existing forms and new forms coming on the way:

Old Forms:

The following forms are fairly old, and we all know and deal with them every year. There are slight changes affecting them to reflect the compliance and requirements of Affordable Care Act (ACA) tax wise.

Form 1040

Form 1040, 1040A, and 1040EZ are the heart of the individual income tax file. Any extra tax or extra credit will be the up and down heartbeat. So, the Premium Tax Credit will show in the 1040 on the Tax and Credit section as more taxes if you receive extra credit through you Marketplace/Exchange allowed Advanced Premium Tax Credit (APTC) or extra credit for you if you didn't utilize your Premium Tax Credit at all or use part of it and you deserve more credit.

The Shared Responsibility Payment is an extra tax that will show in the Other Tax section on form 1040, probably in an added line to that section.

To figure out the PTC or SRP amount, there are two new forms added to form 1040.

Form W-2

As one of the most popular forms when it comes to income tax, this form will share part of the new law reporting. The IRS requires employers who provide health insurance benefits to their employees to report the value of those employer paid health benefits on form W-2 which will appear on box 12 using code "DD".

As an employee, this reporting won't affect your income tax liability as it's just an informational item to the IRS from the employers.

JOSEPH A. GABRA, CPA

New Forms

Although it is not final yet, at the moment I am writing this book, the IRS is working on issuing a couple of forms to facilitate health coverage reporting, determining eligibility for PTC, eligibility for exemption of SRP, or the amount of them. I will classify the forms under two main groups: Reporting and Eligibility & Calculation.

Reporting Forms:

Like the forms 1099 series reporting method, a new series of forms 1095 are coming on the way. These forms will work as informational reports from the source you obtain your health insurance coverage for you and the IRS.

Form 1095 – A

On the individual level, this form will be used to report certain information to the IRS about family members who enroll in a qualified health plan through the Marketplace/Exchange. Form 1095-A also is furnished to individuals to allow them to claim the premium tax credit and reconcile the credit on their returns with advance payments of the premium tax credit (advance credit payments) and to file an accurate tax return. So the early bird tax filers who receive W-2 forms and file their taxes will have to wait for their Marketplace/Exchange to send them Form 1095-A by January 31 of each year. If you do not receive your

1095-A by that date, contact your agent or find your copy through your own marketplace account documents to get this form and include it with your tax documents.

Form 1095 – B

Those who didn't buy their insurance through the Marketplace/Exchange but went directly to the insurance company of their choice, or those who have a Grandfathered plan and still keep their coverage should expect to receive your Form 1095-B no later than January 31 of each year to accompany your tax documents and confirm your participation in health coverage and avoid the SRP, while the insurance companies will report it to the IRS as well at a later date.

Form 1095 – C

Finally in the Form 1095 series, every employer who offers health coverage to their employees and their dependents is required to report on Form 1095-C every detail on this coverage. However this is not required for tax year 2014 or 2015 but it will be enforceable starting tax year 2016; the year which all employers with 50 or more full time employees are required to offer health coverage to their employees or face a penalty.

That topic I will explain in detail in our next edition of this book series for small businesses and large companies.

Eligibility & Calculation

This new forms category that will enable taxpayers to lay out the details about their coverage (first to determine their tax credit eligibility or exemption, and also the calculation of the credit or the payment amount these forms) are as follows:

Form 8962

Premium Tax Credit PTC: this new form will be used to determine the exact amount of your household PTC and also reconcile the amount you already received during the year using the information furnished to you by the Marketplace/Exchange (Form 1095-A). If there is any extra credit you received or you are due, either amount will appear in the Tax and Credit section of Form 1040.

Form 8965

Health Coverage Exemption HCE: The purpose of Form 8965 is to report an exemption granted by the Marketplace/Exchange or to claim a coverage exemption on your tax return. This form will allow you to indicate any month you or another member of your tax household does not have Minimum Essential Coverage.

If you were not qualified for an exemption and didn't have the MEC, that form will be used to determine the Shared

Responsibility Payment (SRP) will show in the OTHER TAXES section of the 1040 form Line 61. Just check the box to indicate whether you have health coverage for the entire year. If you have not, you will use the new form for determining the exemption or calculation of tax penalty.

CHAPTER 10

Practical Cases

On this chapter I will give examples of real questions and actual cases regarding ACA related tax matters.

Case # 1

My income is under the limit and I'm a healthy person with minor issues I take care of through over-the-counter drugs. **Is it a problem if I don't sign onto the exchange?**

Not at all. At the end of the year, based on your income, there will be no penalty on your income tax. In the case of an emergency during the year, you will be covered through your state Medicaid after they consider your income level to be low enough. However, it is a better option to sign onto the exchange and thereby give yourself peace of mind by spending a couple of minutes to enroll yourself online and secure the coverage in advance.

You may seek free professional help through any Certified Agents or Certified Counselors.

Case # 2

With over $3000 monthly home mortgage, $200 auto and home insurance, property tax, credit card, loan, and other obligations, I found the monthly premium will cost more than I can afford based on my financial situation. **Do I still have to enroll while I'm not able to afford to pay the premium?**

Maybe. You need to consult your accountant to study your financial situation to see whether it can be construed as under a hardship condition; in that case, you don't have to apply if you choose not to.

Case # 3

My employer offers optional health insurance benefits. If I don't enroll, I can receive extra payments in my paychecks because of my low income. I have my family coverage under Medicaid. **Does the IRS ask me to pay back these benefit? And do I have to apply for health insurance coverage through Obama Care?**

No. Formally, you have health coverage through your state Medicaid based on your household income. The IRS will not ask you to pay back the extra amount you receive from your employer; it is not extra Premium Tax Credit. The extra payment you received is an extra job benefit included on your W-2 form, and you pay your tax due.

Case # 4

I'm single person making about $30,000/ year. My employer offers health coverage, and I didn't buy any coverage either through my employer or through the Marketplace/Exchange. I thought Obama Care wouldn't make it through, knowing that my employer coverage premium cost less than 8% of my income. **Will I be Liable for Shared Responsibility Payment (SRP)?**

Yes, you will be liable for SRP for 2014 tax year and the calculation could be as follows:

$30,000 - $10,150= $19,850* 1%= **$198.50**. This amount is greater than the $95 flat amount and less than the $2448 NABPP.

Case # 5

We are family of four, and we bought a plan through the exchange during the year. Due to a mistake from the insurance company, our insurance was discontinued and we lost 7 months of coverage. **Will I be Liable for Shared Responsibility Payment (SRP)?**

No. In a case like this there should be no SRP. You or your agent need to contact the Marketplace/Exchange, prove the issue, and obtain a waiver certificate for your household from the exchange.

Case # 6

As usual I didn't apply for my employer plan. The enrollment ended on June 30, 2013, but I enrolled next year. My plan starts on July 1, 2014. Do I pay a penalty? **Will I be Liable for Shared Responsibility Payment (SRP)?**

Maybe. It depends upon the cost of your premium. You can try to obtain your exemption through IRS. You need first to contact a Certified Agent to find out the cost without tax credit to see if it exceeds the 8% threshold. If there is no exemption available for you, you will be required to pay SRP for 6 months only.

Case # 7

I was out of the country for five months, and by the time I came back open enrollment was ended; do I still pay SRP? **Will I be Liable for Shared Responsibility Payment (SRP)?**

Maybe. You still need to get an exemption for those five months. Remember, coming back into the country is considered a special event, and you should be consulting a Certified Agent at that time and obtaining coverage. Consult your accountant as well, as you might be eligible for the 8% Threshold exemption based on the amount of your gross income.

Case # 8

We are family of two persons. One of us has health coverage through an employer. The other individual got confused about the exchange pricing, with one agent telling us the premium cost was $150 monthly. We found later it only cost $10 through the exchange calculator. It ended up that we didn't participate at all this year. **Will I be Liable for Shared Responsibility Payment (SRP)?**

Yes. One person is still liable for SRP simply because he has no coverage. The confusion over pricing is not an excuse, and if you complete your application yourself, you will end up with the same result as your agent. The calculator you are using may not be accurate, especially with some complicated household situations. Trust your agent; he is more aware regarding facts in the exchange system.

Case # 9

We are family of three, and our premium after the tax subsidy came to be $180/month which was still considered a heavy load on our budget especially with the cost of housing and child care expenses. **Can we drop the health insurance?**

Yes, if you are willing to pay the Shared Responsibility Payment of an average of 1% of your household income divided by 12 times the number of months without coverage and carry out the risk of being without insurance. Can you find out how much your auto and home insurance cost you? The real question is, **is it worth it to live without health insurance?**

Case # 10

I learned that someone split their household and did a separate application for the non-working spouse to receive Medicaid. If that is the case, then I can save about $400 on my monthly premium. **Is that an option?**

Not at all. That could be considered fraud. Unless they are Legally Separated, it will never work that way because husband and wife file their tax either Joint or Separate. For the reason of health insurance through the Marketplace/Exchange the separate filers will lose their eligibility for tax credit while Medicaid/MediCal is asking about the tax filing statutes.

We should fill out our Marketplace/Exchange application in the same way we file our income tax. So a married couple should be included in the same application for health insurance, and the income should be that of the household regardless of whether it is coming from one working spouse or two.

Case # 11

My spouse's employer offers coverage for employees' families; I didn't enroll by September 2014 as usual because it's really costly. I enrolled through the Marketplace/ Exchange while waiting for the next employer enrollment. **Will the IRS ask me to pay back the Premium Tax Credit I received?**

Not sure. We don't have that guideline yet as it is the first year of implementation, and many unique issues have not been addressed. Also your case and similar ones are for the partial year of 2014, and it will never happen again. The start of ACA by the end of 2013 didn't give warning to all those who skipped employer enrollment before October 2013. Let's wait for the IRS decision regarding that matter.

Case # 12

We are three single brothers ages from 27 to 35 living in the same home with our mother and supporting her living. **Can we apply together in one application as one household?**

Yes, if. . . . Only if you are all included in one income tax file, meaning one person is the high earner, supports more than 50% of the cost of living for the others, they can be listed as dependents on his file, and all the household members can be included in one file. That is certainly a rare situation.

We need to look at the way how you filed your taxes last year. Remember the prediction characteristic: We need to predict if we are still planning to file the same way next year.

If each one of you files his own return, each one will apply as a single household except one who will file as head of household adding the mother as a dependent on his income tax. So that person will include his mother on his health insurance application.

CONCLUSION

Before Obama Care, the economic analysis recorded that 60% of bankruptcies were related to medical costs. Also, about 50 million people in America were without any medical coverage just because of the cost of carrying health coverage. Healthcare reform has been due for a long time, and finally it is the law of the land. Yes, it's not perfect, but it is the dream of the majority. It is a good start, and we all can participate in improving whatever needs to be improved to eliminate weakness and deficiency.

Now as we all abide by the law, we have to have a better understanding and a clear awareness regarding the implementation of that law which affects important aspects in our life: Healthcare and Income Tax.

The healthcare reform under ACA comes one year ahead of income tax filing. Thus, Certified Insurance Agents can help you now, and in a year your tax accountant will inquire about your health insurance situation.

When you decide if you are going to participate in health coverage or opt out, you need to understand the tax consequences to build your decision on solid ground. You should be in contact with your tax professional when you decide to get healthcare coverage and continue your relationship with your Certified Insurance Agent when your household income changes during the year.

I focused in this book on individual income tax impacts which are coming soon in the 2014 tax season. Taxpayers who made a wrong decision still have time to correct their actions before February 15, 2015, the end of enrollment period on their Marketplace/Exchange. If you prepare your tax file after February 15, then it might be late and you may need to wait another year to correct problems with your healthcare coverage and the impacts they may have on the next year's tax file.

GLOSSARY

Adjusted Gross Income (AGI):

One of the main figures in your tax file where you add all your gross income during the year from all sources and deduct allowable expenses, so called "above the line" deductions.

Advanced Premium Tax Credit (APTC):

An early payment of the premium tax credit in advance to lower the out-of-pocket monthly premium payment and secure the affordability of the health insurance coverage.

Affordable Care Act (ACA):

A short name of healthcare reform act presented by President Obama and signed as law on March 23, 2010.

Certified Insurance Agent (CIA):

An insurance agent trained and certified by the state or federal Marketplace/Exchange to help, educate, and enroll the public in their Marketplace/Exchange.

Donut Hole:

The area where Medicare participants are financially responsible for the cost of Medicare Part D drugs, which is the coverage gap between the initial coverage limit and the catastrophic coverage threshold.

Employer Coverage Level

The percentage of the premium cost for the lowest plan for the employee compared with his combined household income. If it is above 9.5%, it will allow the employee to drop the employer plan and shop through the Marketplace/Exchange with the eligibility of the Premium Tax Credit.

Exemption Certificate Number (ECN):

The certificate a taxpayer or authorized representative requested and received from the Marketplace/Exchange for an individual (Marketplace/Exchange-Granted Coverage Exemptions for Individuals) to be reported on Form 8965.

Federal Facilitate Exchange (FFE)

(www.healthcare.gov) Is a Marketplace/Exchange initiated by the Federal government to help facilitate residents' healthcare coverage enrollment on the states didn't adopted the practice of the law or their own marketplace is not ready yet.

Federal Poverty Line (FPL):

A certain level of income amount considered to be a poverty level for the year based on the household size. The Department of Health and Human Services (HHS) determines federal poverty line amounts annually while the government adjusts the income limits annually for inflation and cost of living. This line varies from state to state.

Flat Dollar Amount:

One of the comparison levels in the Shared Responsibility Payment (SRP) calculation for those who didn't have Minimum Essential Coverage (MEC) during the year and did not qualify for any exemption.

Health Coverage Exemption (HCE):

Name of new tax form 8965 included in form 1040 to report the exemption or calculate the Shared Responsibility Payment.

Household:

For the purposes of the health insurance and premium tax credit, household size includes the all individuals for whom the taxpayer can claim personal exemption deduction on the tax return (e.g., taxpayer, spouse, children, parents, and other dependents).

Marketplace/Exchange:

An administrative governmental entity (state- or federal-based) that approves and facilitates qualified health insurance plans and enrollment.

Minimum Essential Coverage (MEC):

MEC is the lowest level of health insurance coverage a person needs to have during any given year to avoid paying a penalty at year end. After ACA most insurance plans in the Marketplace/Exchange include MEC.

Modified Adjusted Gross Income (MAGI):

When we start with the AGI and re-adjust or modify it adding or subtracting other figures, the new figure is MAGI. There are two main MAGI:

- Taxable MAGI to calculate Alternative Minimum Tax AMT.

- Healthcare MAGI to calculate your household income for Premium Tax Credit eligibility, Shared Responsible payment, and Medical eligibility.

National Average Bronze Plan Premium (NABPP):

The average premium cost of lowest tier plan level "Bronze" nationwide. Used for the purpose of calculation of Shared Responsibility Payment (SRP) as a final, maximum limit.

Obama Care:

A proposal for United State healthcare reform presented by President Obama. Passed the Senate on December 23, 2009, and the House on March 21, 2010. Formally known as the Patient Protection and Affordable Care Act (PPACA).

Patient Protection and Affordable Care Act (PPACA):

New health care reform act signed as law by President Obama in March 23, 2010, known publicly as Obama Care because of the initial proposal of the law presented by the President.

Premium Tax Credit (PTC):

New (refundable) income tax credit used to subsidize health insurance premium payments by the federal government. Taxpayers' income under 400% of FPL may qualify them for that credit.

Shared Responsibility Payment (SRP):

The amount of payment the individual will be required to pay in case he didn't maintain health coverage during the tax year and is not qualify for exemption under any circumstances.

Unaffordable coverage:

The coverage considered to be unaffordable if the individual's premium cost is more than 8% of the household income. In that level you are exempt from paying the penalty if you choose not to get coverage.

REFERENCE

HR360 Blog. (2014, August 7). IRS Issues Guidance on Federal Appeals Court Rulings Regarding ACA Tax Credits https://www.hr360.com/Blogs/HealthCareReform.aspx?id=8659&blogid=839962